P9-BJG-557

AWESOME VACATIONS

CONTENTS

BEACH HUTS

Greetings from Earth! Glax, an alien tourist from outer space, has begun his holiday. He starts with a trip to something called "The Beach," a sandy desert next to a large expanse of water. Humans must be partly solar-powered, because they sure enjoy lying out in the sun! Build a stretch of beach for your vacationing minifigures to enjoy.

Brown bush pieces look like dry beach plants

REAR VIEW

HOME ON THE SAND

At a beach hut, vacationers can change into bathing suits, grab a snack, or snooze in the shade. To make one, build a small one-room house with lots of seaside details. Include a sandy beach around it!

Rows of slopes and jumper plates create a festively striped roof

Transparent slopes in the roof let the sunlight in

A key from the back of a wind-up LEGO® Minifigures character doubles as a latch

Hinged door hatch for a simple storage hut

A LEGO® chain helps the hut's owners pull the open door back down

THIS IS ONE WAY TO GET OUT OF DOING THE WASHING UP!

I THINK WE LEFT THIS FISH OUT IN THE SUN TOO LONG.

Sand bank can be filled with pieces of any shape and color, and then covered with tan plates or bricks

Window pieces without glass support the porch railing

Supports let huts sit level on top of a steep sand bank

Stack up round bricks and plates to build a minifigure-sized sand castle

Build up mounds of plates to make the beach bumpy and uneven

FRONT VIEW

A tile with a number identifies the vacation hut

SURF HUT

The surfers who own this hut have cheered it up by painting a mural on the back wall. Inside are shelves for their surfboards and clips to hold their favorite beach gear.

Mural is built on a small plate and attached to the interior wall using bricks with side studs

HUT CONSTRUCTION

Try building each hut as a separate mini-scene and then connecting their sections of beach together. They can be identical buildings in different colors, or totally individual designs.

Include beach accessories like shells, fishing poles, and swimming equipment

A small ladder provides quick and easy access

Tell a story with your scene. These surfers have just returned from a fishing trip in their rowboat. Time for a beach cook-out!

QUICK BUILD

MICRO BEACH HUT

A big beach hut may take a while to assemble, but you can put together a micro-scale version in no time at all. When you've finished, build even more to make a whole ocean-view scene!

A bracket allows the doors to be attached sideways

Use jumper plates to center the roof slopes

Build matching shapes with different doors and decorations

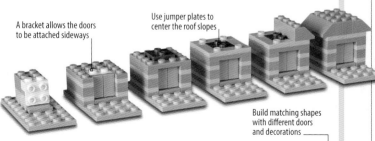

ICE-CREAM STALLS

While at the beach, Glax samples a unique human delicacy: a wafer rolled into a cone and filled with a frozen substance that has something to do with Earth cows. Believe it or not, it tastes much better than it sounds! Who doesn't love sweet, cold ice cream on a sunny day? Build a stall so your beach-goers can enjoy some of their own!

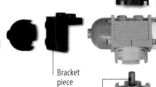

Bracket piece

Long rod

Hinge cylinder underneath the ice-cream sign snaps onto the back of the kiosk

ACK! BRAIN FREEZE!

Big scoops are 2x2 domes in different colors

Alternate curved bricks of the same shape to make a striped awning for the stall's roof

Transparent elements look like glowing lights

Arch is supported by columns built from 1x1 round bricks and plates

This ice-cream scoop started out as a LEGO® Ninjago™ nunchuk handle!

1x1 round plates underneath give the awning a fringe

SMALL KIOSK

This stall is just big enough for a vendor and a freezer full of frozen treats. Give it a bright color scheme and an eye-catching sign overhead, as well as a shade to block the sun on hot summer days.

1x1 round plates make good single-serving scoops

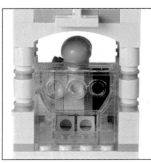

FREEZER

Inside the stall is a freezer full of ice-cream flavors. If you don't have this single transparent piece, you can build your own out of LEGO windows, tiles, and hinge pieces.

Build in textured bricks for detail

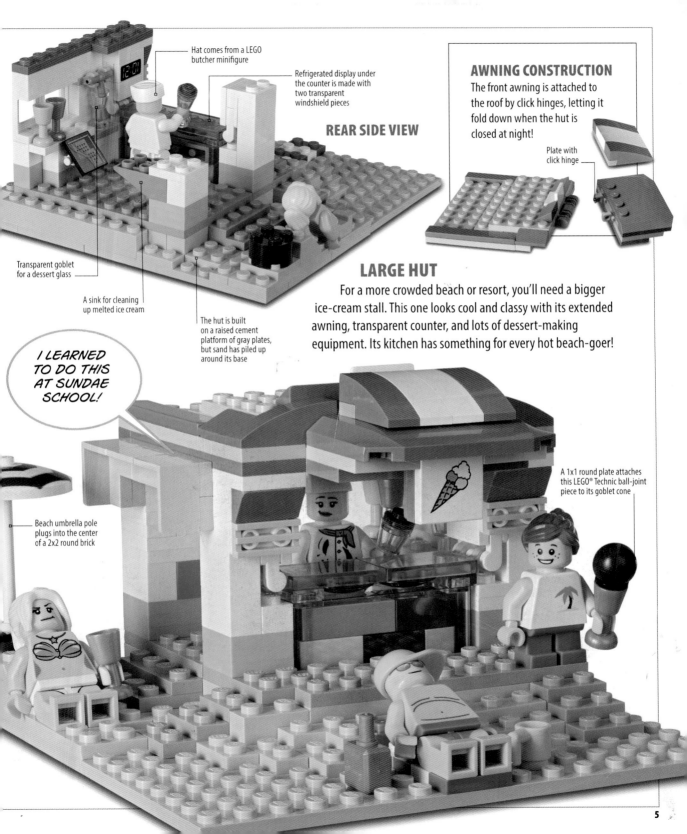

Hat comes from a LEGO butcher minifigure

Refrigerated display under the counter is made with two transparent windshield pieces

REAR SIDE VIEW

AWNING CONSTRUCTION
The front awning is attached to the roof by click hinges, letting it fold down when the hut is closed at night!

Plate with click hinge

Transparent goblet for a dessert glass

A sink for cleaning up melted ice cream

The hut is built on a raised cement platform of gray plates, but sand has piled up around its base

LARGE HUT
For a more crowded beach or resort, you'll need a bigger ice-cream stall. This one looks cool and classy with its extended awning, transparent counter, and lots of dessert-making equipment. Its kitchen has something for every hot beach-goer!

I LEARNED TO DO THIS AT SUNDAE SCHOOL!

A 1x1 round plate attaches this LEGO® Technic ball-joint piece to its goblet cone

Beach umbrella pole plugs into the center of a 2x2 round brick

BEACH BOATS

Glax observes some humans going out on the water inside small floating crafts that lack even basic antigravity propulsion. Perhaps this is an activity that he should attempt as well? Going out in a boat turns a trip to the beach into an adventure on the water, whether you're going fast or taking your time. Build one and try it out!

There are lots of other pieces that can substitute for this rectangular bar element

Auto mudguards create seats with comfy armrests

BOTTOM VIEW

I LIKE THE VIEW.

AND I LIKE THE EXERCISE!

PADDLE BOAT

A paddle boat moves when you turn its foot pedals. The more you pedal, the faster it goes! Build a paddle boat to be flat and stable for a comfortable ride. With two seats, friends can team up for twice the boating fun.

FRONT VIEW

PEDAL POWER

The pedals are round bricks with fins from a rocket. They are connected together by a LEGO Technic cross-axle that passes through a pair of bricks-with-holes so the pedals can spin.

Curved bricks cover and hide the rotating pedal function

Use plates to lock the bricks-with-holes together on the top and bottom

Cross-axle

Pedal

A car roof is a simple way to make the front of the boat, but you could build it out of plates instead

Use long inverted curve bricks to make floatation pontoons

Try building a spinning paddle-wheel under the boat, or one on each side!

Fire fighter hose nozzles plugged into jumper plates give the passengers something to hold onto

Black tooth-shaped piece resembles a banana's stem— or use a 1x1 cone or round brick

1x1 slopes fill in the gaps on the sides

Not enough yellow pieces? Add spots, or make a green, red, or over-ripe brown banana instead!

A long plate on the bottom locks it all together

BANANA BOAT

Get creative with your boat designs. You could make a boat that looks like a hot dog, a dolphin...or a giant yellow banana! Use slopes and inverted slopes to make the body, and big and small cones for the ends.

UNDER THE PEEL

Brackets provide the sideways studs that hold the cone-shaped ends of this model in place, but you could use other pieces for the same effect, such as headlight bricks or LEGO Technic cross-axles.

Leave 1x2 gaps in the top of the boat for minifigures

WHOA! THIS IS ONE SLIPPERY BANANA BOAT!

Bracket piece

Side floats are stacks of round bricks held together by rods, and attached to plates with side rings

QUICK BUILD

Minifigure has room to sit or stand

Handle piece attaches to a robot claw plugged into a click-hinge cylinder

Steering controls can turn left or right and adjust up or down

JET-SKI

Here's a small but speedy model that you can put together in a flash. Build it in any colors you like and get ready for a wet and wild ride!

NOW THIS IS MY KIND OF SKI VACATION!

Grille slopes for rear vents

Curved surfaces with few studs blast through wind and waves

Use plates to add a stripe on the side

HOTEL POOL

After Glax's beach adventure, he discovers a building where individual hibernation pods can be rented for the night. Amazingly, it includes its own miniature ocean! A hotel swimming pool provides even more opportunities for vacation fun. Your minifigures can swim, splash, play water-tag, and even take a leap from the high diving board!

SWIMMING POOL

Build a big swimming pool for a vacation hotel! You can make rippling water by adding layers of transparent blue pieces over a base of blue plates. Include other familiar pool features, such as a diving board and a lifeguard. If you don't have enough pieces to build an entire pool, just make part of one!

Binoculars and a floatie ring are a lifeguard's most important gear

Place the lifeguard's seat on a raised platform so he can spot any trouble

NO FAIR. WHY CAN'T I GO FOR A SWIM TOO?

HEY MOM, BOBBY IS MAKING BUBBLES!

Use 1x2 wall elements to make ladder steps

Use small tiles and round plates to create waves

Attach the top half of a minifigure to the water surface to make it look like he is submerged in water!

I HOPE EVERYBODY DOWN THERE IS READY FOR A BIG SPLASH!

You could also build hand-rails with bricks or clips and bars

Clip a ladder to the back of the board so your minifigures can climb up to the top

Build pool signs with letter and number tiles

Coat the board with tiles— or leave two studs exposed at the end so you can attach a diving minifigure

An angled support beam makes a good base for a sturdy diving board

Try building a big splash under the diving board!

Build the water into the pool walls to keep everything locked together

Look through your collection for pool-side accessories such as balls, swim fins, and beach umbrellas.

SUN LOUNGERS

Build your hotel guests some sun lounger chairs so they can kick back, relax, and catch a few rays by the pool. There are lots of different ways to make them!

WHERE'S THE "HOVER" BUTTON ON THIS THING?

Angled back—use a hinge to make it adjustable

Seat is low to the ground

Build a lounger with or without armrests

MAKING A SPLASH

Glax's afternoon at the pool has left him soaked. He tries to dry himself by using a rapid-velocity acceleration ramp, but that only results in him becoming wetter! Make a towering waterslide and send your minifigures screaming with laughter into the water below.

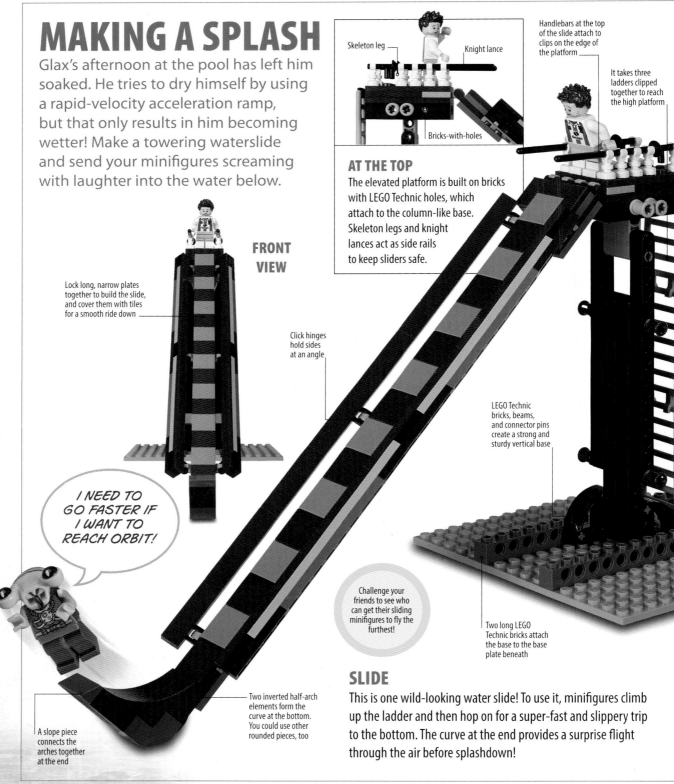

Skeleton leg

Knight lance

Handlebars at the top of the slide attach to clips on the edge of the platform

It takes three ladders clipped together to reach the high platform

Bricks-with-holes

AT THE TOP
The elevated platform is built on bricks with LEGO Technic holes, which attach to the column-like base. Skeleton legs and knight lances act as side rails to keep sliders safe.

FRONT VIEW

Lock long, narrow plates together to build the slide, and cover them with tiles for a smooth ride down

Click hinges hold sides at an angle

LEGO Technic bricks, beams, and connector pins create a strong and sturdy vertical base

I NEED TO GO FASTER IF I WANT TO REACH ORBIT!

Challenge your friends to see who can get their sliding minifigures to fly the furthest!

Two long LEGO Technic bricks attach the base to the base plate beneath

A slope piece connects the arches together at the end

Two inverted half-arch elements form the curve at the bottom. You could use other rounded pieces, too

SLIDE

This is one wild-looking water slide! To use it, minifigures climb up the ladder and then hop on for a super-fast and slippery trip to the bottom. The curve at the end provides a surprise flight through the air before splashdown!

SURFBOARDS

Surfboards come in lots of different sizes—though you probably haven't seen too many like this! There are official minifigure-scaled LEGO surfboard elements, but you can also build your own out of plates, boat parts, and other long, flat, and curved pieces.

WHOA. THESE ARE SOME RIGHTEOUS BOARDS, DUDE!

The long, curved pieces at the front and back come from airplane, boat, helicopter, and spaceship sets

The bigger you make your surfboard, the more colors and patterns you can build into it

TOP VIEW

TOP VIEW

Use tiles for smooth, flat surfaces on top

A LEGO Technic connector pin connects this fin piece to a plate-with-hole on the board's underside

The bottom of this board uses rectangular, angled, and even circular plates

The size of these surfboards is determined by the size of the special parts on the ends

TOP VIEW   **BOTTOM VIEW**

BOTTOM VIEW

★ *CHALLENGE*

BAGGAGE CART STACKER

Have you ever tried to cross a busy airport with a cart full of luggage? Build a simple base with wheels, add a brick to it, and roll it over to a friend, who adds another brick and rolls it back with a single push. Who will be the first to topple the truck?

Construct ramps and obstacles for an even bigger challenge!

Can you place your bricks in a way that makes your opponent's bricks off-balance?

Try building rolling bases of different shapes, or using different-sized wheels

BENEATH THE SEA

Diving under the sea is like exploring a whole different world. The fish remind Glax of some of his friends back home! Whether you're diving from a speedboat on the surface or swimming down near the sea floor, you're sure to see scenery and animals that you've never encountered before when you venture beneath the waves.

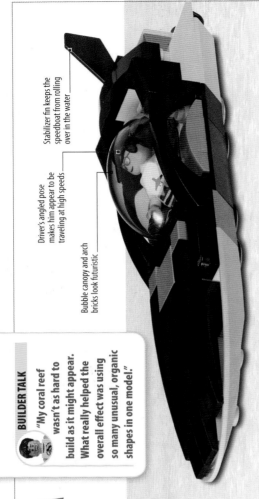

Stabilizer fin keeps the speedboat from rolling over in the water

Driver's angled pose makes him appear to be traveling at high speeds

Bubble canopy and arch bricks look futuristic

LUXURY SPEEDBOAT

For the ultimate in sea thrills, build a super-fast speedboat and hang on tight! Long curved and inverted-curve bricks make this boat's nose look smooth and streamlined. Give your speedboat a big engine and a windshield to protect the driver from water spray.

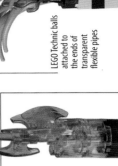

LEGO Technic balls attached to the ends of transparent flexible pipes

REAR VIEW

Use transparent pieces for taillights

BOTTOM VIEW

Place round sliding plates on the bottom to coast across flat surfaces!

CLEVER CORALS

Coral structures should look unique. This one is built by clipping transparent blue ax heads onto a rod sticking out of a stack of 2x2 round bricks.

Use tentacles to create long, waving sea plants

Brown bar piece

Blue brush head

SCHOOL DAYS

Build a floating school of fish by clipping them above a bar piece using robot or skeleton arms. Create even stranger ocean life with brushes from a LEGO® Friends set!

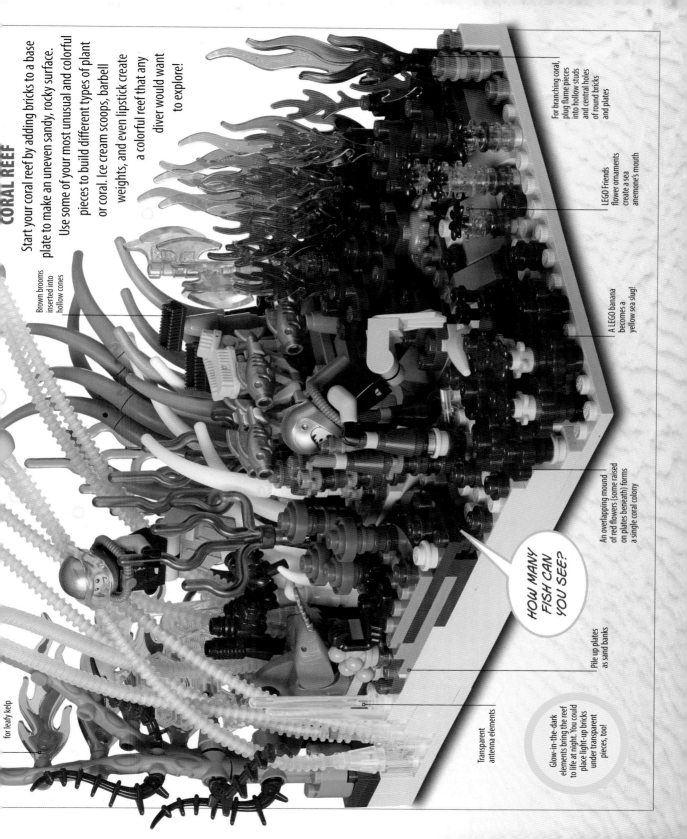

CORAL REEF

Start your coral reef by adding bricks to a base plate to make an uneven sandy, rocky surface. Use some of your most unusual and colorful pieces to build different types of plant or coral. Ice cream scoops, barbell weights, and even lipstick create a colorful reef that any diver would want to explore!

Brown brooms inserted into hollow cones

for leafy kelp

Transparent antenna elements

HOW MANY FISH CAN YOU SEE?

Glow-in-the-dark elements bring the reef to life at night. You could place light-up bricks under transparent pieces, too!

Pile up plates as sand banks

An overlapping mound of red flowers (some raised on plates beneath) forms a single coral colony

A LEGO banana becomes a yellow sea slug!

LEGO Friends flower ornaments create a sea anemone's mouth

For branching coral, plug flame pieces into hollow studs and central holes of round bricks and plates

EXTREME SPORTS

Glax thinks he has finally discovered how humans get into orbit. They climb up mountains! For a real rugged outdoor adventure, try a day of rock-climbing— or let your minifigures do it for you! You can give them an extra thrill by building a bungee jump up at the top!

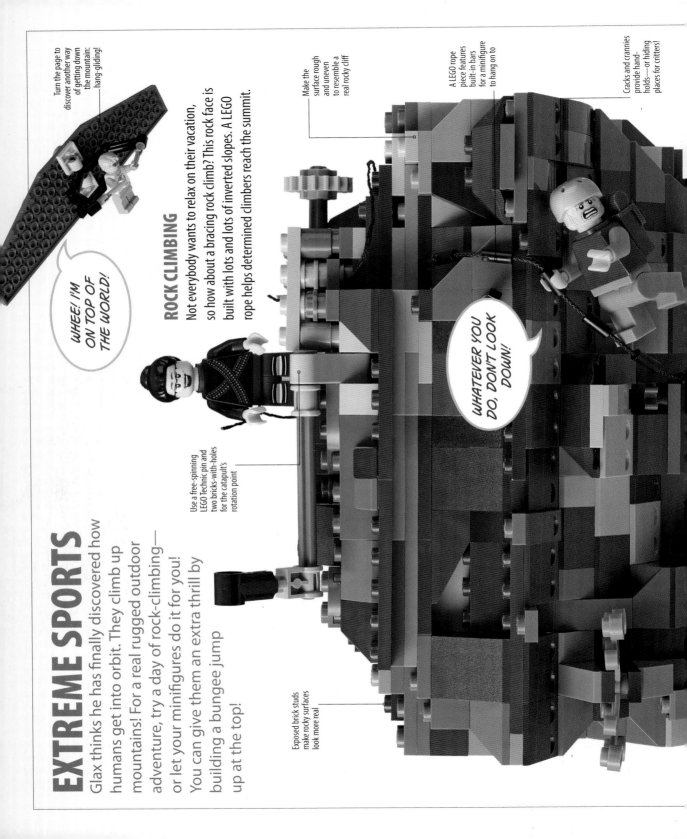

Turn the page to discover another way of getting down the mountain: hang-gliding!

WHEE! I'M ON TOP OF THE WORLD!

ROCK CLIMBING

Not everybody wants to relax on their vacation, so how about a bracing rock climb? This rock face is built with lots and lots of inverted slopes. A LEGO rope helps determined climbers reach the summit.

Make the surface rough and uneven to resemble a real rocky cliff

A LEGO rope piece features built-in bars for a minifigure to hang on to

Cracks and crannies provide hand-holds—or hiding places for critters!

WHATEVER YOU DO, DON'T LOOK DOWN!!

Use a free-spinning LEGO Technic pin and two bricks-with-holes for the catapult's rotation point

Exposed brick studs make rocky surfaces look more real

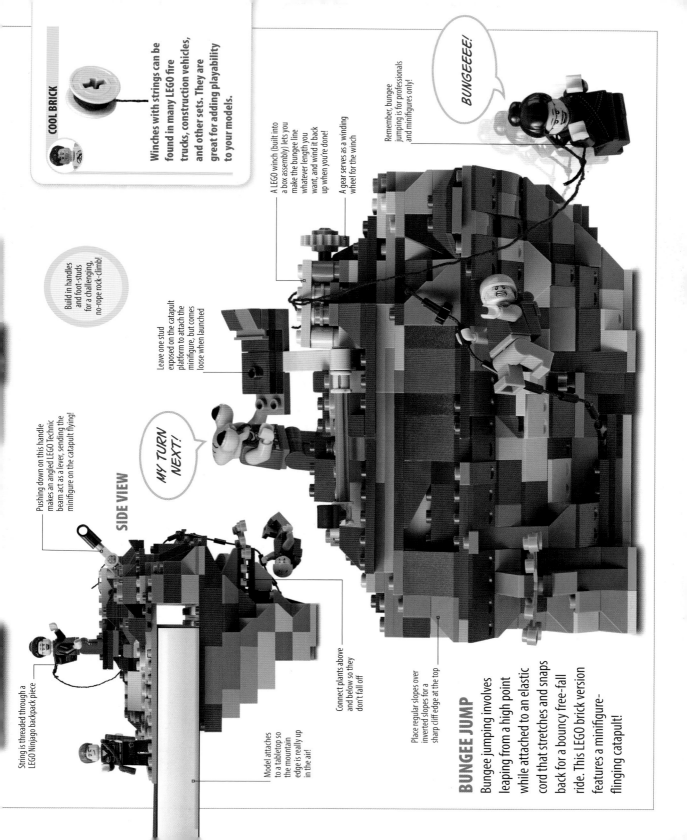

Winches with strings can be found in many LEGO fire trucks, construction vehicles, and other sets. They are great for adding playability to your models.

BUNGEEEE!

Remember, bungee jumping is for professionals and minifigures only!

A LEGO winch (built into a box assembly) lets you make the bungee line whatever length you want, and wind it back up when you're done!

A gear serves as a winding wheel for the winch

Leave one stud exposed on the catapult platform to attach the minifigure, but comes loose when launched

Build in handles and foot-studs for a challenging, no-rope rock-climb!

SIDE VIEW

MY TURN NEXT!

Pushing down on this handle makes an angled LEGO Technic beam act as a lever, sending the minifigure on the catapult flying!

String is threaded through a LEGO Ninjago backpack piece

Model attaches to a tabletop so the mountain edge is really up in the air!

Connect plants above and below so they don't fall off

Place regular slopes over inverted slopes for a sharp cliff edge at the top

BUNGEE JUMP

Bungee jumping involves leaping from a high point while attached to an elastic cord that stretches and snaps back for a bouncy free-fall ride. This LEGO brick version features a minifigure-flinging catapult!

ADVENTURES UP HIGH

These humans cannot seem to decide whether they want to go up or down. Not only do they climb and bounce, but they even strap on wings and fly! Send your minifigures to even greater heights by building entire mountains for them to scale, and colorful hang gliders to help them sail safely back down to the ground below.

A long LEGO Technic pin at the top center attaches the frame to two plates-with-holes, one in front and one behind

THIS IS SO MUCH FUN, I MIGHT NEVER COME BACK DOWN...

Main glider wing is made with two large, mirror-image angled plates

Thanks to the LEGO Technic pin connection, the harness frame can swing left and right as the minifigure pilot shifts weight to steer

HANG GLIDER

Help your vacationing minifigures see the sights from a bird's-eye view with a hang glider! Gliders are much smaller and easier to build than full airplanes. All you need is a flat wing surface and a way for a pilot to hang on beneath.

MINIFIGURE MOUNTAIN

Let's hope your minifigures aren't afraid of heights, because they're going on an exciting mountaineering vacation! Use basic bricks to build a tall mountain—then take turns against your friends to race your minifigures to the top. To make your minifigures' mountain climb even more of a challenge, you could use small colored pieces as distance markers, stopping your minifigures only at points of the same color.

Use white bricks for a snow-capped peak

Where in the world is your mountain located? Use different colors to create brown desert cliffs, green jungle slopes, or black and red volcanoes.

Small, colored pieces make distance markers

Build your mountain as tall as you want it to be!

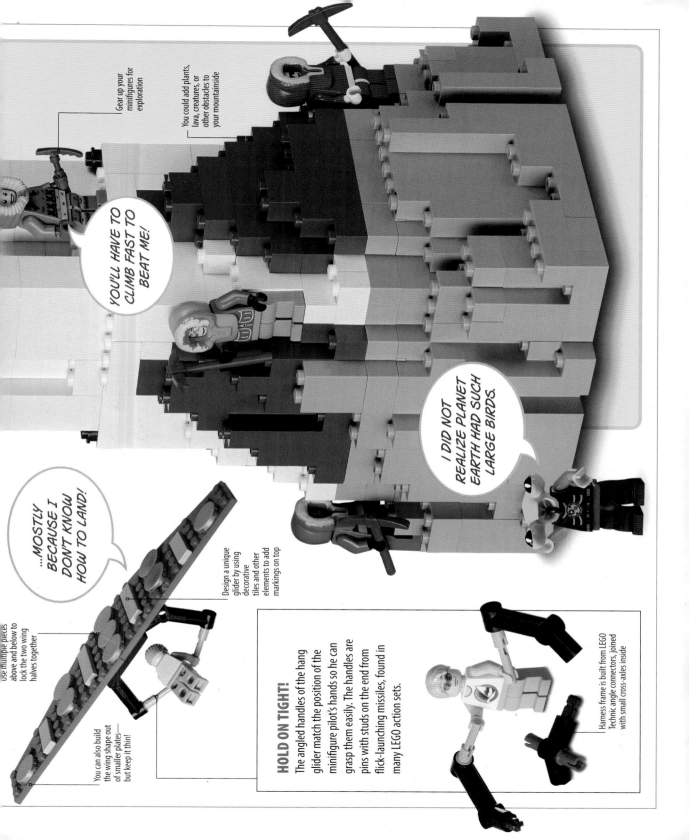

MOUNTAIN BIKING

How can Glax get back down from the mountain? He looks for a jetpack vendor, but instead finds a friendly Earthling who trades a foot-powered, two-wheeled contraption for Glax's favorite disintegrator blaster. Do you have a few LEGO bicycles? Then build a bumpy, rocky dirt path down the mountain for them to ride and race along!

Include small round and square pieces for pebbles and other outdoor details

BIKE TRACK

Turn LEGO bicycles into mountain bikes by building an outdoor track for them to race on. Make the track as big or small as you like, and add stunt features such as ramps, pits, and obstacles to steer around.

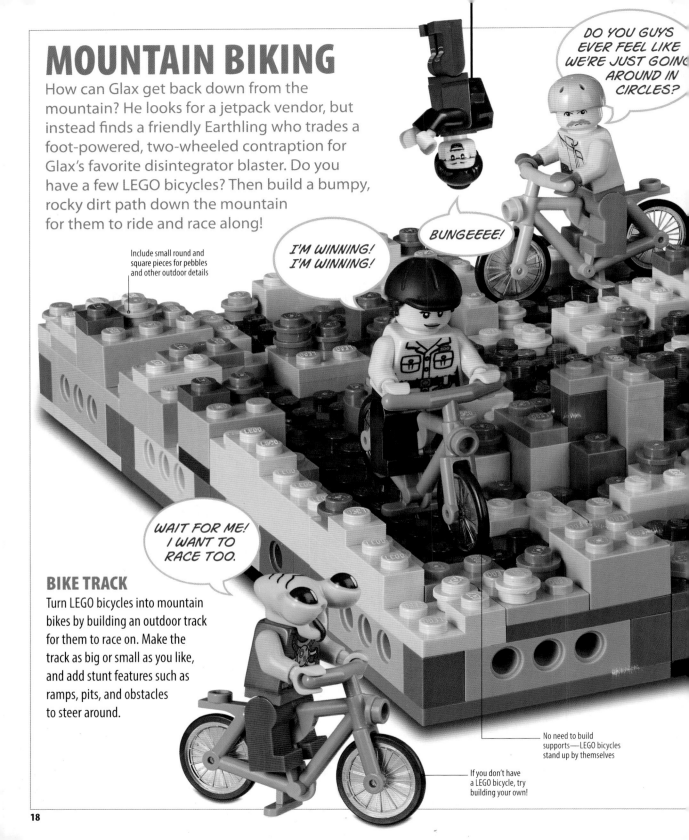

No need to build supports—LEGO bicycles stand up by themselves

If you don't have a LEGO bicycle, try building your own!

Sturdy headgear is important when biking, especially on uneven terrain

WHEE!

TRACK LAYOUT

To make your track interesting, vary your paths—make straight lines, tight corners, T-junctions, crossroads, zig-zags, and dead ends. You could also include growing plants, fallen tree trunks, and narrow streams or even rivers for the bikes to jump over!

Raised plates in the same color as the trail create a realistic surface

Rearrange the sections to build a new course!

Use brown plates to make dirt trails

Consider building part of your trail out of slope bricks and racing your bikes to the bottom!

CONNECTING YOUR COURSE

To make a modular bike course, construct each section on a 6x6 plate with 1x4 LEGO Technic bricks on their sides. Connect the sections with LEGO Technic pins so that their paths line up to create a complete track.

If you don't have enough 1x4 LEGO Technic bricks, use two 1x2 ones instead

Since the middle will be covered, you can use any colors you want!

Fill in the corners with 1x1 bricks

WATER ADVENTURES

When the humans talked about "white water rafting," Glax did not expect to be floating down a rushing river at high speeds, narrowly avoiding many large rocks. This is even better than asteroid-surfing! Build a big raft or a kayak and send your most daring minifigures on a thrilling ride through the rapids.

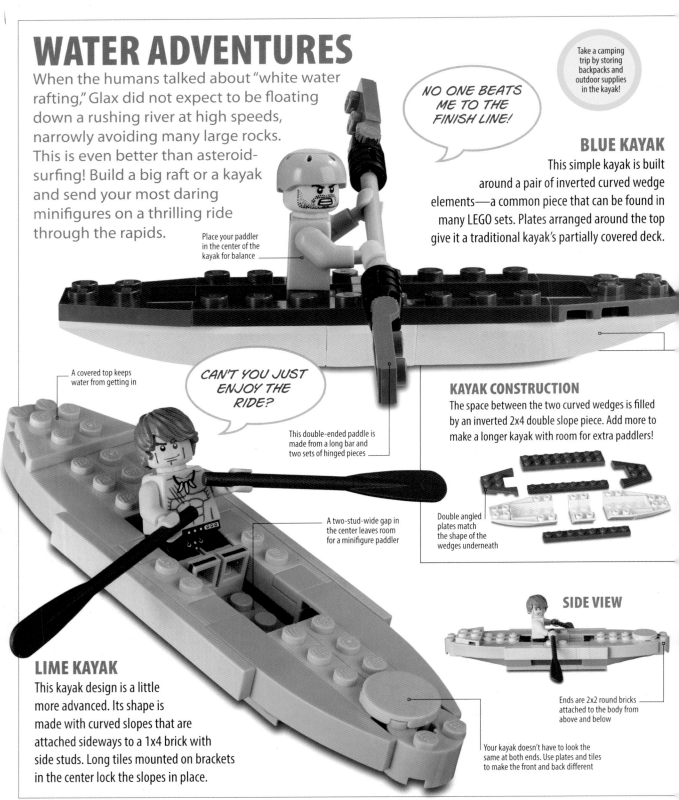

Take a camping trip by storing backpacks and outdoor supplies in the kayak!

NO ONE BEATS ME TO THE FINISH LINE!

Place your paddler in the center of the kayak for balance

BLUE KAYAK

This simple kayak is built around a pair of inverted curved wedge elements—a common piece that can be found in many LEGO sets. Plates arranged around the top give it a traditional kayak's partially covered deck.

A covered top keeps water from getting in

CAN'T YOU JUST ENJOY THE RIDE?

This double-ended paddle is made from a long bar and two sets of hinged pieces

KAYAK CONSTRUCTION

The space between the two curved wedges is filled by an inverted 2x4 double slope piece. Add more to make a longer kayak with room for extra paddlers!

A two-stud-wide gap in the center leaves room for a minifigure paddler

Double angled plates match the shape of the wedges underneath

SIDE VIEW

LIME KAYAK

This kayak design is a little more advanced. Its shape is made with curved slopes that are attached sideways to a 1x4 brick with side studs. Long tiles mounted on brackets in the center lock the slopes in place.

Ends are 2x2 round bricks attached to the body from above and below

Your kayak doesn't have to look the same at both ends. Use plates and tiles to make the front and back different

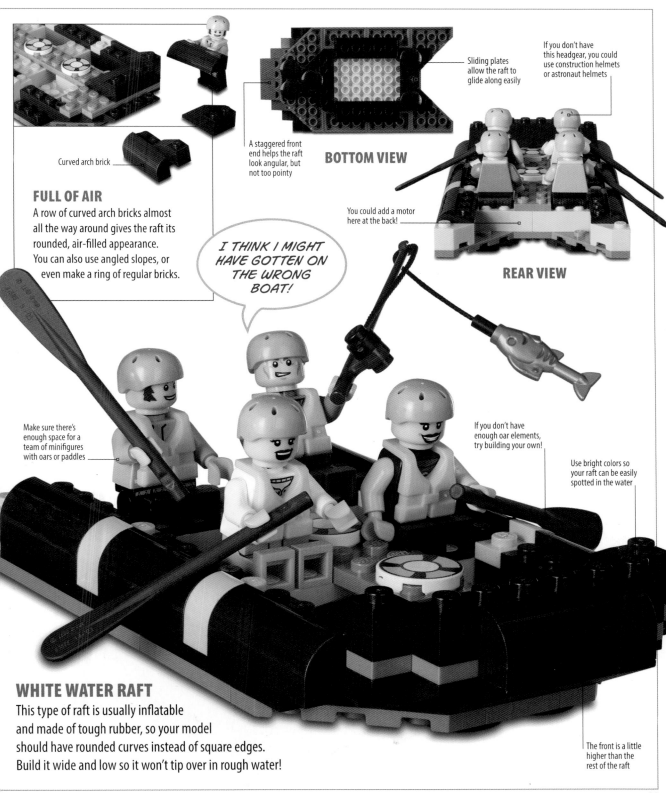

Curved arch brick

A staggered front end helps the raft look angular, but not too pointy

BOTTOM VIEW

Sliding plates allow the raft to glide along easily

If you don't have this headgear, you could use construction helmets or astronaut helmets

You could add a motor here at the back!

REAR VIEW

FULL OF AIR

A row of curved arch bricks almost all the way around gives the raft its rounded, air-filled appearance. You can also use angled slopes, or even make a ring of regular bricks.

I THINK I MIGHT HAVE GOTTEN ON THE WRONG BOAT!

Make sure there's enough space for a team of minifigures with oars or paddles

If you don't have enough oar elements, try building your own!

Use bright colors so your raft can be easily spotted in the water

WHITE WATER RAFT

This type of raft is usually inflatable and made of tough rubber, so your model should have rounded curves instead of square edges. Build it wide and low so it won't tip over in rough water!

The front is a little higher than the rest of the raft

SKIING

It may look like ice cream, but Glax finds Earth snow much less tasty, especially without chocolate syrup on top. On the other hand, it's great for skiing! Equip your minifigures with skis or snowboards and build them a snowy slope to slide down.

Carry your skiers up to the top in an electric cable car and let the cold-climate adventures begin!

> ERM… I WAS HANG-GLIDING, BUT NOW I'M JUST HANGING.

Cable is a flexible LEGO tube, but you can use a long bar or even a string!

Bricks and plates with click hinges create a bent armature between the roof and the cable

Big windows will let your passengers see the snowy landscape

Use a printed tile for the ski resort's logo

If you don't have this piece you could use a window or a windscreen instead

BUILDER TALK

"If you're making a tall, sloped surface like a ski run, make sure you add filler bricks to support it from inside. Otherwise, you might have an avalanche on your hands!"

STAY CONNECTED

A plate with side ring provides a secure connection and lets the cable car slide up and down the tube—or use a clip instead!

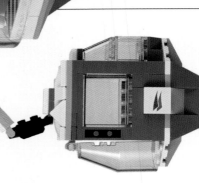

Plate with side ring

CABLE CAR

Build an enclosed cable car to carry multiple minifigures up the slopes. It should be lightweight and sturdy enough to hang from the cable without coming apart. Add bricks inside so your skiers have benches to sit on, and leave plenty of space for skiing gear.

Add white pieces to the roof for a coating of snow

Hinged spaceship canopy door opens to let skiers get on and off

A tile with caution stripes says "Watch your step!"

SKI SLOPE

You can build a ski slope of any size and shape—from an easy nursery slope for beginners to a steep mountainside for fearless experts. Find all of the white slope bricks in your collection and start building!

You could attach curved bricks to make gentler, more rounded snowdrifts.

If you don't have minifigure skis and ski poles, improvise! Use long, thin plates to make skis, and rods or anything skinny with a handle for the poles

LEFT-SIDE VIEW

Sharp peaks look like mountains far off in the distance

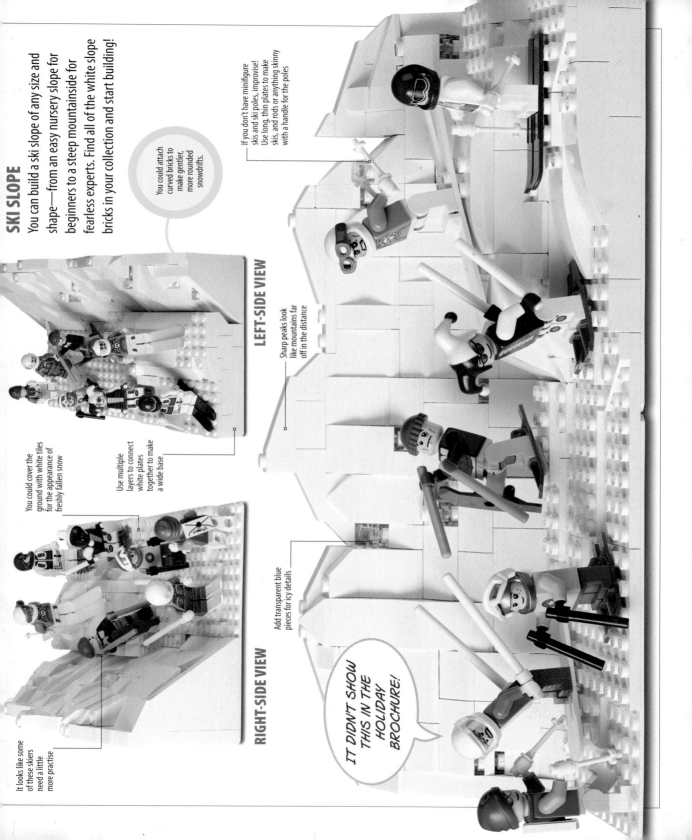

You could cover the ground with white tiles for the appearance of freshly fallen snow

Use multiple layers to connect white plates together to make a wide base

RIGHT-SIDE VIEW

Add transparent blue pieces for icy details

IT DIDN'T SHOW THIS IN THE HOLIDAY BROCHURE!

It looks like some of these skiers need a little more practise

SNOW TRANSPORTS

What's the best way for an alien tourist to trek around on a snow-covered mountain? Earth technology has provided visitors with several useful options. Whether they choose to drive through the drifts on a snowmobile or surf down the slopes on a snowboard, it's a whole lot easier than using snow shoes to get where you need to go!

SNOWMOBILE

Who needs roads? When you have a snowmobile, you can go anywhere...as long as it's covered in snow! Give your snowmobile skis in front for steering, and a treaded tire in back for traction and power.

SIDE VIEW

Attach a four-stud-wide front end to a three-stud-wide back with jumper plates

A bracket lets you attach these curved bricks using sideways building

A clipped-on flap keeps snow from spraying on anyone behind the snowmobile!

Short minifigure skis are held by faucet elements, which plug into 1x1 plates with side rings on the snowmobile

A long, free-spinning LEGO Technic pin holds the tire in place

A hinge plate holds the controls at a comfortable angle

Use latticed elements to form a railing to keep the riders in place—or use regular 1x4 bricks

2x12 plate attaches to 1x4 bricks with side studs on the base

Strings attach to the outermost studs on 1x4 bricks with side studs

Curve made from four arch pieces attached to a 1x4 plate

TOBOGGANS

A toboggan is the perfect snow transport. It's fun, fast, and you can fit a few minifigure friends aboard it if you make yours long enough. You need a wide, flat base, an upwards-curving front, spots for riders to sit or stand, and strings for steering.

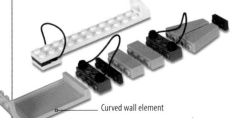

Curved wall element

SIDEWAYS SLIDER

The J-shaped nose of this toboggan is made from a tall, curved wall element. Most of the rest is built sideways, from a combination of bricks, plates, and slopes.

SNOWBOARD JUMP

It's like surfing on a frozen wave! Give your snowboarding minifigures something to really jump about by building a snowy-looking stunt ramp. Assembling the slope is relatively easy, but the curve at the bottom may take a bit of clever construction.

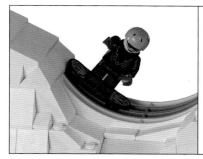

HALF-PIPE

This stunt, the half-pipe, was built by connecting four large arches side-by-side with tiles and plates with clips. They attach to the rest of the snowboarding model upside-down!

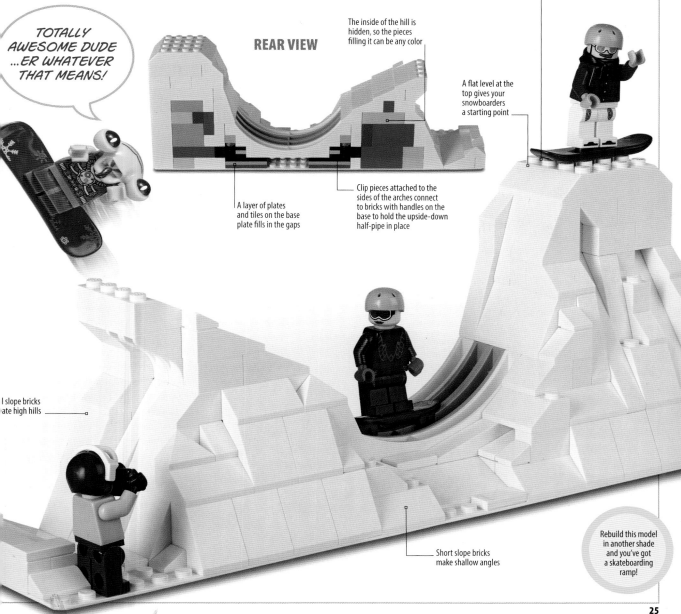

TOTALLY AWESOME DUDE ...ER WHATEVER THAT MEANS!

REAR VIEW

The inside of the hill is hidden, so the pieces filling it can be any color

A flat level at the top gives your snowboarders a starting point

A layer of plates and tiles on the base plate fills in the gaps

Clip pieces attached to the sides of the arches connect to bricks with handles on the base to hold the upside-down half-pipe in place

l slope bricks ate high hills

Short slope bricks make shallow angles

Rebuild this model in another shade and you've got a skateboarding ramp!

SKI HOTEL

Skiing may not be as cold as wading through the nitrogen streams of Pluton IV, but it's still nice to have somewhere to warm up at the end of a long day on the slopes. Build a lodge where your winter vacationers can relax and thaw out by the fire. If you're lucky, Glax won't have finished off all of the hot chocolate!

ALPINE HOTEL

Before you start building, do some planning. Pick out doors and windows you would like to use (or you could construct your own), and choose colors that look good together. Don't forget to think about the little details that will bring your hotel to life!

The undersides of bricks add their own interesting effects

Use white slopes to make a snow-covered rooftop

Windows with shutters help keep out the cold

Clips in the wall ho ornamental bars

Fence elements can also be a terrace's railing

Auto mudguards make good arches over windows

Plates between brick layers add decoration and support

ALL THIS SHOVELING SURE KEEPS YOU TOASTY!

A lamppost with a telescope base helps late arrivals find their way to the front door

Stack extra white plates for deeper snow on the ground

Shovel the entrance so you door has enoug clearance to swing open!

HOTEL-BUILDING

If you only assemble the front of the hotel, you can keep the back open to move your minifigures around the different rooms and floors. Make sure the bottom floor is strong so that it doesn't fall apart as you add the higher levels.

Build in a peaked roof for a traditional Alpine-style building

HOME COMFORTS

Your hotel will need some amenities to keep the vacationers happy. Include things like chairs, telephones, cabinets, a fireplace, and a hatstand for storing hats and ski equipment.

You can store all kinds of odd objects up in the attic!

Looks like this bat has found somewhere warm to stay for the winter!

The split flue carries smoke from the fireplace on the middle floor to the chimneys on the roof

Pillars and inverted slopes help bear the weight of the structures above them

Transparent yellow 1x1 round plates create soft interior lights

...ack log ...ricks to make ...additional ...g columns ...nd walls

Include a magazine rack in reception!

HANDFUL OF BRICKS LIST

4x4 plate x 1

2x2 inverted slope x 1

2x2 brick x 3

2 x 4 brick x 2

2x2 plate x 2

1x2/1x4 angle plate x1

1x6 plate x 2

2x2 slope x 3

Antenna x1

1x2 slope x 2

2x3 slope x 1

1x1 slope x 4

1x1 brick eyes x 2

1x2 tile with top bar x 1

1x2 plate x 1

1x1 round brick x 1

2x4 angled plate x 2

1x3 brick x 2

1x2 curved half-arch x 1

4x4 round plate x 1

2x2 round brick x 1

DK | Penguin Random House

For DK Publishing
Project Editor Hannah Dolan
Senior Designer Guy Harvey
Editors Jo Casey, Matt Jones, Victoria Taylor
Designers Jill Bunyan, Sam Richiardi, Lauren Rosier, Rhys Thomas
Jacket Designer David McDonald
Senior DTP Designer Kavita Varma
Pre-production Producer Siu Chan
Producer Lloyd Robertson
Managing Editor Simon Hugo
Design Manager Guy Harvey
Creative Manager Sarah Harland
Art Director Lisa Lanzarini
Publisher Julie Ferris
Publishing Director Simon Beecroft

For the LEGO Group
Project Manager Mikkel Joachim Petersen
Assistant Licensing Manager Randi Kirsten Sørensen
Senior Licensing Manager Corinna van Delden
Designer Melody Louise Caddick
Building Instruction Developer Alexandra Martin
Model makers Stephen Berry, Yvonne Doyle, Rod Gillies,
Tim Goddard, Tim Johnson, Barney Main, Pete Reid

Photography by Gary Ombler

First published in the United States in 2015 by DK Publishing
345 Hudson Street, New York, New York 10014

Contains material previously published in LEGO® *Play Book* (2013)

001—284611—Mar/15

Page design copyright © 2015 Dorling Kindersley Limited.
A Penguin Random House Company.

Acknowledgments
Dorling Kindersley would like to thank: Randi Sørensen, Mikkel Petersen,
Melody Caddick, Corinna van Delden, and Alexandra Martin at the LEGO Group;
Stephen Berry, Yvonne Doyle, Rod Gillies, Tim Goddard, Tim Johnson, Barney Main,
Pete Reid, and Andrew Walker for their amazing models; Daniel Lipkowitz for his inspiring
text; Gary Ombler for his endless patience and brilliant photography; and Emma Grange,
Lauren Nesworthy, Lisa Stock, and Matt Wilson for editorial and design assistance.

1x1 brick x 7

4x6 plate x 1

1x1 headlight brick x 2

1x4 brick x 6

1x2 brick x 5
(including 1 transparent)

1x6 brick x 2

1x2 jumper plate x 3

2x3 brick x 1

1x1 round plate x 2

1x2x1 panel x1

2x2 radar dish x 2

1x4 plate x 2

1x1 cone x 1

Wide rim, wide tire,
and 2x2 axle plate
with 1 pin x 4

2x6 plate x 3

1x1 plate x 4

1x2 grille plate x 2

2x4 plate x 2

Faucet x 1

1x6 arch brick x 1

2x2 round plate x 2

4x4 radar dish x 1